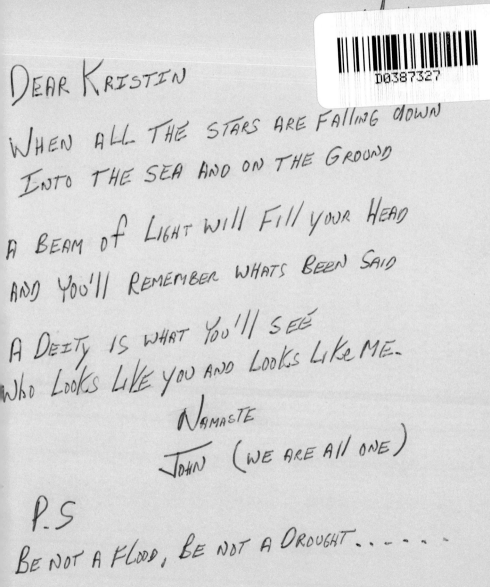

Dear Kristin

When all the stars are falling down
Into the sea and on the ground

A beam of light will fill your head
And you'll remember whats been said

A deity is what you'll see
Who looks like you and looks like me.

Namaste

John (we are all one)

P.S

Be not a flood, be not a drought . . . . . .

POPPOPOMG@AOL

Meditations from A Course in Miracles

Meditations from A Course in Miracles

Inspirational quotes of universal wisdom

BARNES & NOBLE

NEW YORK

Design copyright © 2007 by Ivy Press Limited

This 2007 edition published by Barnes & Noble, Inc.,
by arrangement with Ivy Press

Extracts are taken from the 1975 edition
of *A Course in Miracles,* published by the
Foundation for Inner Peace, Inc.
P.O. Box 598
Mill Valley
CA 94942
USA

ISBN-13: 978-0-7607-9364-0
ISBN-10: 0-7607-9364-6

Printed in China

1 3 5 7 9 10 8 6 4 2

This book was conceived, designed, and produced by
IXOS, an imprint of Ivy Press
The Old Candlemakers, West Street,
Lewes, East Sussex BN7 2NZ, UK

Creative director Peter Bridgewater
Publisher David Alexander
Editorial Director Caroline Earle
Senior Project Editor Hazel Songhurst
Art Director Sarah Howerd
Designer Simon Goggin

Contents

Introduction

The first edition of *A Course in Miracles* was published by the Foundation for Inner Peace in the summer of 1975, and over 30 years later, the single-volume edition continues to sell in large numbers with over one-and-a-half million copies in print. In addition, many thousands of people have attended the courses run by the Foundation for Inner Peace in Temecula, California—an organization founded in 1983 whose purpose was to deepen the understanding of students of the course— and in similar organizations around the world.

In *Meditations from A Course in Miracles* you will find a selection of quotations taken from the original book, which we have organized thematically across eight topics. The book can be read from cover to cover, or it can be dipped into, or accessed via its index, which will direct you to a particular subject.

The course is, in fact, a complete self-study system of spiritual thought that illustrates the path to universal love and peace through a process of forgiveness and by the discarding of all guilt.

Although much of its text is couched in traditional Christian language, its teachings and its message are universal.

How *A Course in Miracles* came into being is a fascinating story. Its authors, Helen Schucman and William Thetford were, in the early 1960s, both Professors of Psychology at Columbia University's College of Physicians and Surgeons in New York City. Both were career-oriented psychologists who would not have thought of themselves as spiritual people. In fact, they were having such difficulty working together that they agreed to find "another way" to resolve the tensions that existed between them.

Very soon afterward, Helen started to have very vivid, sometimes disturbing dreams filled with heightened imagery, psychic episodes and visions. The whole experience began to feel increasingly religious with the figure of Jesus appearing more and more. Throughout her dreams Helen heard an inner voice, and on October 21,1965, this now-familiar voice said to her: "This is A Course in Miracles."

Deeply troubled, Helen telephoned William and they immediately agreed to start writing down what Helen had heard. Helen would dictate what she had dreamed, and William would type it up, a process that they continued daily for seven years. At the end of that time they had completed what is now *A Course in Miracles*, which consists of 669 pages of text, a 488-page Workbook for Students, and a 92-page Manual for Teachers. The course can best be summed up in this simple quote taken from it:

Nothing real can be threatened
Nothing unreal exists
Herein lies the peace of God.

We have found the experience of compiling the book both inspiring and illuminating. We hope that in reading it you will be drawn to discover the vast treasures that lie within the pages of *A Course in Miracles* and that this, in turn, will lead you to find a more miraculous life.

Meditations
on Adversity

On not admitting pain

Nothing can hurt you unless you give it the power to do so.

On the healing power of time

Can you imagine what it means to have no
cares, no worries, no anxieties, but merely
to be perfectly calm and quiet all the time?
Yet this is what time is for; to learn just
that and nothing more.

On the power
of miracles

This world is full of miracles.
They stand in shining silence next
to every dream of pain and suffering,
of sin and guilt. They are the dream's
alternative, the choice of the dreamer,
rather than deny the active role in
making up the dream.

On unlocking the door to Heaven

All you need to do is but to wish that
Heaven be given you instead of hell,
and every bolt and barrier that seems to
hold the door securely barred and locked
will merely fall away and disappear.

On the lessons of life

Trials are but lessons that you failed to
learn presented once again, so where you
made a faulty choice before you now can
make a better one, and thus escape all pain
that what you chose before has brought to you.

Meditations
on Knowledge

On the key to teaching

Every good teacher hopes to give his students so much of
his own learning that they will one day no longer need him.
This is the one true goal of the teacher.

On changing your perspective

. . . seek not to change the world, but choose
to change your mind about the world.
Perception is a result and not a cause.

On avoiding distorting reality

Fantasy is an attempt to control
reality according to false needs.
Twist reality in any way and you
are perceiving destructively.

On having faith as a teacher

A good teacher must believe in the
ideas he teaches, but he must also
meet another condition; he must
believe in the students to whom
he offers the ideas.

On recognizing the value of what you have

What have you taught yourself that you can possibly prefer to keep, in place of what you *have* and what you *are*?

On always remaining open to learning

Those who remember always that they know nothing, and who have become willing to learn everything, will learn it. But whenever they trust themselves, they will not learn. They have destroyed their motivation for learning by thinking they already know.

On remaining true
to your self

All roads that lead away from what you are
will lead you to confusion and despair.

On avoiding temptation

Be vigilant against temptation,
then, remembering that it is but
a wish, insane and meaningless,
to make yourself a thing that you
are not. And think as well upon the
thing that you would be instead.

Meditations on
Universal Truths

On recognizing the holy instant

The holy instant is not an instant of creation,
but of recognition. For recognition comes of vision
and suspended judgement. Then only it is possible
to look within and see what must be there, plainly in sight,
and wholly independent of inference and judgment.

On understanding those less well off

If you have no investment in anything in this world,
you can teach the poor where their treasure is.
The poor are merely those who have invested
wrongly, and they are poor indeed!

On understanding the nature of truth

Truth does not vacillate: it is always true.

Whatever is true is eternal, and
cannot change or be changed.
Spirit is therefore unalterable
because it is already perfect,
but the mind can elect what
it chooses to serve.

On protecting the truth

The best defense, as always,
is not to attack another's position,
but rather to protect the truth.

On the purity of truth

The search for truth is but the honest searching
out of everything that interferes with truth.
Truth *is*. It can neither be lost nor sought nor found.

On sacrifice

For if there is sacrifice, someone must pay and someone must get. And the only question that remains is how much is the price, and for getting what.

On accepting your path through life

Your way is decided.
There is nothing you will not be
told, if you acknowledge this.

On choices

You are free to believe what you choose,
and what you do attests to what you believe.

On looking beyond what your eyes see

Appearances deceive, but can be changed. Reality is changeless. It does not deceive at all, and if you fail to see beyond appearances you *are* deceived.

On avoiding false values

Have faith in nothing and you will find the "treasure"
that you seek. Yet you will add another burden to
your already burdened mind. You will believe that
nothing is of value, and will value it. A little piece of
glass, a speck of dust, a body or a war are one to you.
For if you value one thing made of nothing, you have
believed that nothing can be precious, and that you
can learn how to make the untrue true.

Meditations on
Faith and Prayer

On recognizing the irreconcilable

All magic is an attempt at reconciling the irreconcilable.
All religion is the recognition that the irreconcilable cannot be reconciled.

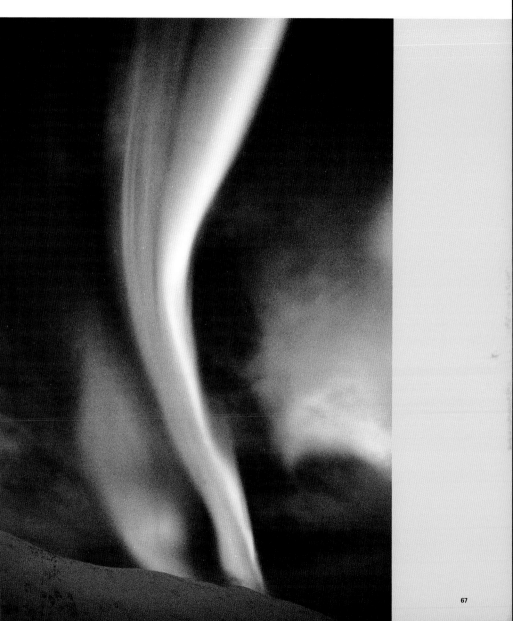

On the folly of asking for things

Everyone who ever tried to use prayer to ask for
something has experienced what appears to be failure.

On looking beyond what you see

Be willing, for an instant,
to leave your altars free of
what you placed upon them,
and what is really there you
cannot fail to see.

On asking for forgiveness

Prayer is a way of asking for something.
It is the medium of miracles. But the
only meaningful prayer is for forgiveness,
because those who have been forgiven
have everything.

BERT J SANDERS · JACK H SHOOP Jr · ARTHUR J SANDERS · LEWIS
UNCAN P SMYLY · JAMES R SPELLER · HARRY E STEPHENS · JAMES E
WIN W VAN ORDEN Jr · DANIEL VARELA · ANTHONY VIGIL · RICHA
ARLES J WATTERS · REMER G WILLIAMS · JOEL S WILLIAMSON · RO
UIS G W ARNOLD · GREGORY C BAUER · BRUCE M BENZING · NEA
BERT T BLY · HARVEY L BROWN III · RICHARD J BUSENLEHNER · DA
MBROSE J CERENE · THOMAS L CORBETT · CLAUDE L CRAWFORD
HN D AGOSTINO · LARRY A D'ENTREMONT · ROBERT P DEGEN
HN M DUNBAR · JAMES C FARLEY · GREGORY S FENNIMORE · MIC
ARLES R CREWS · JUAN M GARCIA · MICHAEL J GLADDEN · HERB
EVEN R POWELL · WILLIAM T HAGERTY · CLARENCE HALL · BOBBY
ILLIAM D HERST III · AARON K HERVAS · KENNETH J JACOBSON
ESTON LANGLEY · CARLOS J LOZADA · ROGER D MABE · JOHN M
ACY H MURREY · JOSH C NOAH · JAMES W NOTHERN
BERT E PACIOREK · THELBERT G PAGE · JOSEPH PANNEL
NNETH A PETERSON · ARNOLD PINN · DENNIS GREENWALD
SSE SANCHEZ · ERNEST R TAYLOR Jr · JOHN W SMITH · ERVIN
ANK E STOKES · ROBERT T SZYMANSKI · JEROME C SHOMAKER
STER TYLER · ERNESTO VILLARREAL · THOMAS J WADE · EARL K WEB
MUEL T WILLIAMS · JOHN R WOLF · JOHN W WOOTEN
NT E BAHNSEN · WILLARD T BATEMAN · WILLIAM A BEAU
ARY M BRIXEY · DAVID L EATON · HAROLD BURTON · RO
AROLD E CUMBIE · FRED R DODE · WILLIE LEE BROADN
ILLIAM C HINKLE · DAVID E HOMMEL · FLOYD A HYDER
DY R LEE · ROBERT W LINDGREN · ROLAND W MANUEL · ROBERT
ARY D MCDONALD · ROBERT L McLEOD · VAUGHN T O NEIL · RAYMOND
VIN A PORTER · JESSE E SMITH · OLIS R RIGBY · JESUS D RIVERA
VID R REYNOLDS · RONALD G SMITH · MICHAEL J SULLIVAN
NLS WILSON · JEROME P WEBER · THOMAS B ALLEN
ONALD W HOLLENBACH · MARSHALL F FRENG · KENNETH E
EVEN · JERRY D JOH

On finding the answer within

Look not to idols.
Do not seek outside yourself.

On remembering
your true purpose

Whenever you are tempted
to undertake a useless journey
that would lead away from light,
remember what you really want . . .

On faithlessness

Yet faithlessness is sickness.
It is like a house set upon straw.
It seems to be quite solid and
substantial in itself. Yet its stability
cannot be judged apart from its
foundation. If it rests on straw,
there is no need to bar the door
and lock the windows and make
fast the bolts. The wind will
topple it, and rain will come
and carry it into oblivion.

Meditations
on Peace

On hiding nothing

When you have become willing to hide nothing,
you will not only be willing to enter into communion
but will also understand peace and joy.

On finding perfect peace

Think not you understand anything
until you pass the test of perfect peace,
for peace and understanding go together
and can never be found alone.

On getting rid of hatred

The blood of hatred fades
to let the grass grow green again,
and let the flowers be all white
and sparkling in the summer sun.

On remaining open-minded

Only the open-minded can be at peace,
for they alone see reason for it.

Meditations on
Forgiveness
and Charity

On understanding the nature of forgiveness

Forgiveness is the end of specialness.
Only illusions can be forgiven, and then they
disappear. Forgiveness is release from all illusions,
and that is why it is impossible but partly to forgive.

On the cost of giving

The cost of giving *is* receiving.
Either it is a penalty from which you suffer,
or the happy purchase of a treasure to hold dear.

On charity

Charity is a way of looking at another
as if he had already gone far beyond
his actual accomplishments in time.
Since his own thinking is faulty
he cannot see the Atonement for himself,
or he would have no need of charity.

On the key to forgiveness

Forgiveness removes only the untrue,
lifting the shadows from the world
and carrying it, safe and sure within
its gentleness, to the bright world
of new and clean perception.

On recognizing
what is important

Recognize what does not matter, and
if your brothers ask you for something
"outrageous," do it because it does not matter.
Refuse, and your opposition establishes
that it does matter to you.

On letting go of the past

Forgive the past and let it go, for it *is* gone.

Meditations on Ego

On understanding the ego

The ego is a wrong-minded attempt
to perceive yourself as you wish to be,
rather than as you are. Yet you can
know yourself only as you are,
because that is all you can be sure of.
Everything else *is* open to question.

On taking selfish decisions

Whenever you choose to make decisions for yourself you are thinking destructively, and the decision will be wrong. It will hurt you because of the concept of decision that led to it. It is not true that you can make decisions by yourself or for yourself alone.

On perception

Perception is the medium by which
ignorance is brought to knowledge.

On negativity of the ego

The ego teaches that Heaven is here and now
because the future is hell. Even when it attacks
so savagely that it tries to take the life of someone
who thinks it is the only voice, it speaks of hell
even to him. For it tells him hell is here as well,
and bids him leap from hell into oblivion.

On justifying hatred

Only the self-accused condemn.

Whatever form his sins appear to take,
it but obscures the fact that you
believe it to be yours, and therefore
meriting "just" attack.

On finding your true function

Every decision you make stems from what you think you are, and represents the value that you put upon yourself. Believe the little can content you, and by limiting yourself you will not be satisfied. For your function is not little, and it is only by finding your function and fulfilling it that you can escape from littleness.

Meditations on Love and Relationships

On the miracle of love

Miracles occur naturally as expressions of love.
The real miracle is the love that inspires them.
In this sense everything that comes from love
is a miracle.

On honoring relationships

It is impossible to use one relationship at the
expense of another and not suffer guilt.
And it is equally impossible to condemn
part of a relationship and find peace within it.

On understanding others

In everyone you see but the reflection
of what you choose to have him be to you.

On love

Love is not learned.
Its meaning lies within itself.
And learning ends when you
have recognized all it is *not*.

Love is not learned,
because there never was a
time in which you knew it not.

On the holy encounter

When you meet anyone,
remember it is a holy encounter.
As you see him you will see yourself.
As you treat him you will treat yourself.
As you think of him you will think of yourself.
Never forget this, for in him you will find
yourself or lose yourself.

Meditations
on **Fear**

On not accepting fear

When you are afraid of anything, you are acknowledging
its power to hurt you. Remember that where your heart is,
there is treasure also. You believe in what you value.
If you are afraid, you are valuing wrongly.

On taking charge
of your fears

The correction of fear *is* your responsibility.
When you ask for release from fear, you
are implying that it is not. You should ask
instead, for help in the conditions that
have brought the fear about.

On finding satisfaction in reality

What can be fearful but fantasy, and
who turns to fantasy unless he despairs
of finding satisfaction in reality?

On Atonement

Miracles represent freedom from fear.
"Atoning" means "undoing."
The undoing of fear is an essential part
of the Atonement value of miracles.

On the lack of necessity for fear

All aspects of fear are untrue because
they do not exist at the creative level,
and therefore do not exist at all.

Meditations
on Time

On understanding the nature of time

Time and eternity are both in your mind,
and will conflict until you perceive time
solely as a means to regain eternity.

Time can release as well as imprison,
depending on whose interpretation
of it you use.

On dreams

You recognize from your own experience
that what you see in dreams you think is real
while you are asleep. Yet the instant you waken
you realize that everything that seemed to happen
in the dream did not happen at all. You do not
think this strange, even though all the laws of
what you awaken to were violated while you
slept. Is it not possible that you merely shifted
from one dream to another, without really waking?

On no coincidences

There are no accidents in salvation.
Those who are to meet will meet,
because together they have the
potential for a holy relationship.
They are ready for each other.

On not being deceived by time

Past, present and future are
not continuous, unless you force
continuity on them. You can
perceive them as continuous,
and make them so for you.
But do not be deceived, and
then believe that this is how it is.

On not banking on future happiness

Be not content with future happiness.
It has no meaning, and is not your just reward.
For you have cause for freedom *now*.

On wasting time

Time can waste as well as be wasted.

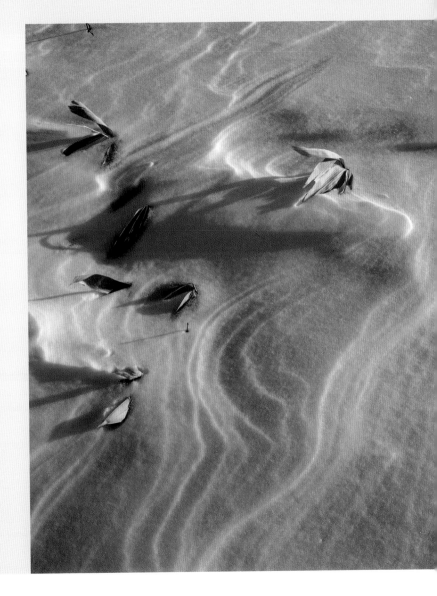

On changing the past

How can you change the past except in fantasy?
And who can give you what you think the past
deprived you of? The past is nothing.
Do not seek to lay the blame for deprivation on it,
for the past is gone. You cannot really not let go
what has already gone.

Index

Acknowledgments

The publisher would like to thank the following people and organizations for the use of images in this book.
Every effort has been made to acknowledge the pictures, however we apologize if there are any unintentional omissions.

Corbis 2 (Hans Strand), 13 (Markus Moellenberg/zefa, 15 (David Vintiner/zefa), 17 (David Fokos), 19 (Pat O'Hara), 25 (Bob Krist), 27 (Pablo Corral Vega), 29 (Anthony Redpath), 35 (Tamara Reynolds), 39 (Stefan Schuetz/zefa), 43 (Bill Ross), 47 (Charles O'Rear), 49 (Ron Sanford), 55 (Michael Amendolia), 57 (Kazuyoshi Nomachi), 59 (Gary Braasch), 61 (B.S.P.I.), 63 (Ben Welsh/zefa), 73 (Craig Lovell), 79 (David Katzenstein), 107 (Steven Vote), 109 (LaCoppola & Meier/zefa), 113 (Nik Wheeler), 115, 119 (Robert Essel NYC), 125 (Elisa Lazo de Valdez), 135 (Joe McBride), 137 (Annie Griffiths Belt), 141 (Arthur Morris).

Getty Images 23 (Val Loh), 31 (Sisse Brimberg), 33 (24-7 Dave Hansen/America), 41 (Angela Wyant), 45 (Nicho Sodling/Johner Images), 51 (Elena Segatini/Iconica), 69 (Joseph Devenney), 71 (Darren Robb), 75 (Keystone), 85 (Eliot Elisofon/Life), 97 (Atli Mar Hafsteinsson/Nordic Photos), 101 (Helena Karlsson), 103 (Kai Tirkkonen/Gorilla), 121 (Sami Sarkis), 123 (Tim Flach), 127 (Alistair Berg), 131 (Hy Peskin), 145 (Neil Overy/Gallo Images), 147 (Frank Walsh).

iStockphoto 53 (Rosemarie Gearhart), 87 (Nikola Bilic), 129 (Gustaf Brundin), 133 (Freder).

Jupiter Images 7, 9, 37, 77, 89, 91, 111, 139, 143, 149.

Johanna Ljungblom 83.

Scott Stoked 81.